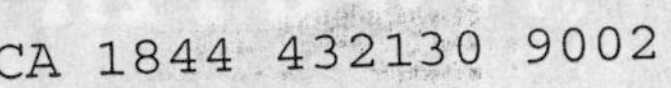

Oil in the Middle East

John King

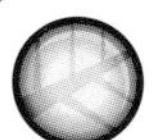

www.raintreepublishers.co.uk
Visit our website to find out more information about **Raintree** books.

To order:
Phone 44 (0) 1865 888112

Send a fax to 44 (0) 1865 314091

Visit the Raintree bookshop at **www.raintreepublishers.co.uk** to browse our catalogue and order online.

Produced for Raintree by
Monkey Puzzle Media Ltd.
Gissing's Farm, Fressingfield
Suffolk IP21 5SH, UK

First published in Great Britain by Raintree,
Halley Court, Jordan Hill, Oxford OX2 8EJ,
part of Harcourt Education.
Raintree is a registered trademark of Harcourt Education Ltd.

Edited by Jenny Siklós and Paul Mason
Designed by Tim Mayer
Picture Research by Lynda Lines and Frances Bailey
Production by Duncan Gilbert
The consultant, Dr. Robert Stern, works as a part-time analyst for the US State Department, primarily as part of the War on Terror. He is a former Associate Director for Counter-Terrorism.

Originated by Modern Age
Printed and bound in China by South China Printing Company Ltd

10 digit ISBN 1 844 43207 6 (hardback)
13 digit ISBN 978 1 844 43207 3 (hardback)
10 09 08 07 06 05
10 9 8 7 6 5 4 3 2 1

10 digit ISBN 1 844 43213 0 (paperback)
13 digit ISBN 978 1 844 43213 4 (paperback)
11 10 09 08 07 06
10 9 8 7 6 5 4 3 2 1

British Library Cataloguing in Publication Data
King, John, 1939-
Oil in the Middle East. - (The Middle East)
1.Petroleum industry and trade - political aspects - Middle East - Juvenile literature 2.Middle East - Foreign economic relations - Juvenile literature 3.Middle East - History - 20th century - Juvenile literature 4.Middle East - Foreign relations - Juvenile literature 5.Middle East - Economic conditions - 1945- - Juvenile literature
I.Title
956'.05

Acknowledgements
The author and publisher are grateful to the following for permission to reproduce copyright material: AKG-Images p. **15**; Corbis pp. **1** (Françoise de Mulder), **6** (Georgina Bowater), **10** (Hulton-Deutsch Collection), **18** (Bettmann), **23** (Bettmann), **25** (Bettmann), **28** (Françoise de Mulder), **34** (Suhaib Dalem/Reuters), **36** (Michel Setboun), **42** (Dept. of Defense/Reuters), **45** (Shamil Zhumatov/ Reuters), **47** (Tom Wright/Skyscan); Getty Images pp. **4** (Allen Tannenbaum), **9** (Hulton Archive), **11** (Central Press/Hulton Archive), **13** (Fox Photos), **16** (Dmitri Kessel/Time & Life Pictures), **17** (Dmitri Kessel/Time & Life Pictures), **20** (Hulton Archive), **21** (Dmitri Kessel/Time & Life Pictures), **26** (AFP), **27** (Ted Thai/Time & Life Pictures), **32**, **33** (Thomas Hartwell/Time & Life Pictures), **35** (Joe Raedle), **39** (AFP), **40** (Barry Iverson/Time & Life Pictures), **41** (Adam Jan/AFP), **43** (Bilal Qabalan/AFP), **46** (Justin Sullivan), **53** (Spencer Platt); Network Photographers p. **31** (Peter Jordan); Reuters p. **38** (Morteza Nikoubazl); Rex Features p. **29** (SIPA); Topfoto.co.uk pp. **5** (Peter Gleizes/UNEP), **8**, **12**, **14**, **22**, **24**, **30**.

Cover photograph shows an Iraqi policeman guarding an oil pipeline that had been sabotaged near Karbala in 2004 (Reuters/Faleh Kheiber).

Map illustrations by Encompass Graphics Ltd.

Every effort has been made to contact copyright holders of any material reproduced in this book. Any omissions will be rectified in subsequent printings if notice is given to the publishers.

The paper used to print this book comes from sustainable resources.

Contents

Some words are shown in **bold**, like this. You can find out what they mean by looking in the Glossary.

The Burning Oil Wells of Kuwait

"Occupying territory by force is unacceptable. No one, friend or foe, should underestimate our determination to confront aggression. America does not seek conflict. But America will stand by her friends."
(US President George H. W. Bush after the invasion of Kuwait)

Oil is an extremely precious resource to humanity. Industries, businesses and people all around the world depend on oil for energy. But oil is found in relatively few places. Because of this, it is the reason for many conflicts, in the Middle East and elsewhere.

In August 1990, the Middle Eastern country of Iraq, led by Saddam Hussein, invaded the small neighbouring country of Kuwait. The motive behind the attack was oil. Iraq was desperate for cash, and wanted Kuwait's valuable oil resources. Iraq also claimed that Kuwait really belonged to Iraq.

The USA quickly said that Iraq should not be allowed to keep Kuwait. It then led an international allied force of 500,000 troops to neighbouring Saudi Arabia, ready to attack the Iraqis. In February 1991, the Iraqi forces were finally driven from Kuwait by the US-led **alliance**.

A US soldier scans the horizon as forces of the US alliance move to expel Iraqi forces from Kuwait.

REASONS FOR IRAQ'S ATTACK ON KUWAIT

- **Iraq borrowed money from Kuwait during the Iran-Iraq war (1980–1988). Saddam Hussein did not believe he should be asked to pay this back.**
- **Iraq said that Kuwait was producing too much oil. This made the price of oil cheaper and so Iraq made less money from its own oil.**
- **Iraq accused Kuwait of taking Iraqi oil from an oilfield on the border between the two countries.**

As they fled, the Iraqis carried out a planned operation to set Kuwait's 613 oil wells on fire. Black smoke billowed up from the flaming wellheads, shutting out the sunlight and turning Kuwait into a nightmare landscape. It would be more than eight months before all the fires were put out.

Kuwait's oil industry eventually went back into full production, but oil released into the sea and the aftermath of the fires inflicted long-lasting **ecological** damage. Iraq, meanwhile, was placed under **United Nations (UN)** sanctions, and would remain in turmoil until well after the US-led invasion of 2003 that removed Saddam Hussein from power.

Above all, however, the war served as a powerful reminder to the world of the importance of oil, both to the Middle East and the world at large.

A lake of oil spreads to the horizon after fleeing Iraqi forces destroy Kuwaiti wellheads in 1991. Choking fumes were a danger to humans and to the environment.

Why is Middle East Oil So Important?

“The only long-term solution to the problem is to reduce the world's reliance on oil.”
(The Economist magazine, October 2003)

The first oil well was drilled in the USA in 1859. Oil soon became the basic fuel of the modern world. And as the **petrochemical industry** developed, oil began to be used to make many chemical substances, including plastics, fertilizers, dyes and medicines.

Oil first became truly important when the car was invented. From the early 1900s, the automobile industry expanded rapidly in the USA. People loved the freedom that cars brought them. Cars, of course, ran on a form of oil called petroleum. Because petroleum was available cheaply, the car industry grew very quickly. The world was transformed by oil, and oil remains our basic fuel in the 21st century. Our homes, industries and transport all depend largely on oil as a fuel.

Oil is at the heart of life in the Gulf, creating a mix of modern technology and age-old traditions.

The USA itself used to be a major oil producer. In 1939, 60 per cent of the world's oil was produced in the USA. Today the USA's share is significantly less, perhaps as little as 3 per cent of the world's known remaining usable oil resources of around a trillion **barrels**. In 2005 the USA imported around 65 per cent of the oil it used. A fifth of these US oil **imports** came from the Middle East. A quarter of Saudi Arabia's production goes to the USA.

Oil is a 'finite' resource. This means that there is only a certain amount of it in the world. One day our oil will run out. As oil becomes less and less common, its price will rise. Some of the world's oil is in difficult locations and today would be too expensive to extract from the ground. But as our oil starts to run out and prices rise, some of this 'extra' oil may become worth extracting. It is more likely, though, that by then we will have developed alternative fuels to oil.

Meanwhile, the Middle East holds up to 65 per cent of the world's known extractable **oil reserves**. A few experts believe there may be much more oil than we think, especially in South America. Even if this is true, over the next few decades, the Middle East will remain a key source of oil for the whole world. It is this which makes it such an important place.

OIL IN SAUDI ARABIA

Saudi Arabia alone has over a quarter of the world's known oil reserves, with 261 billion barrels. This is important for two reasons. First, the world may come to be more dependent than it is at the moment on Middle Eastern oil. Second, the sheer size of the Saudi reserves gives Saudi Arabia a great deal of influence over the price of oil. If the Saudis decide to produce more oil, the price falls. If they decide to cut back production, oil becomes harder to get hold of and the price rises.

The main oil-producing countries of the Middle East. Small quantities of oil are also found in Egypt and Yemen.

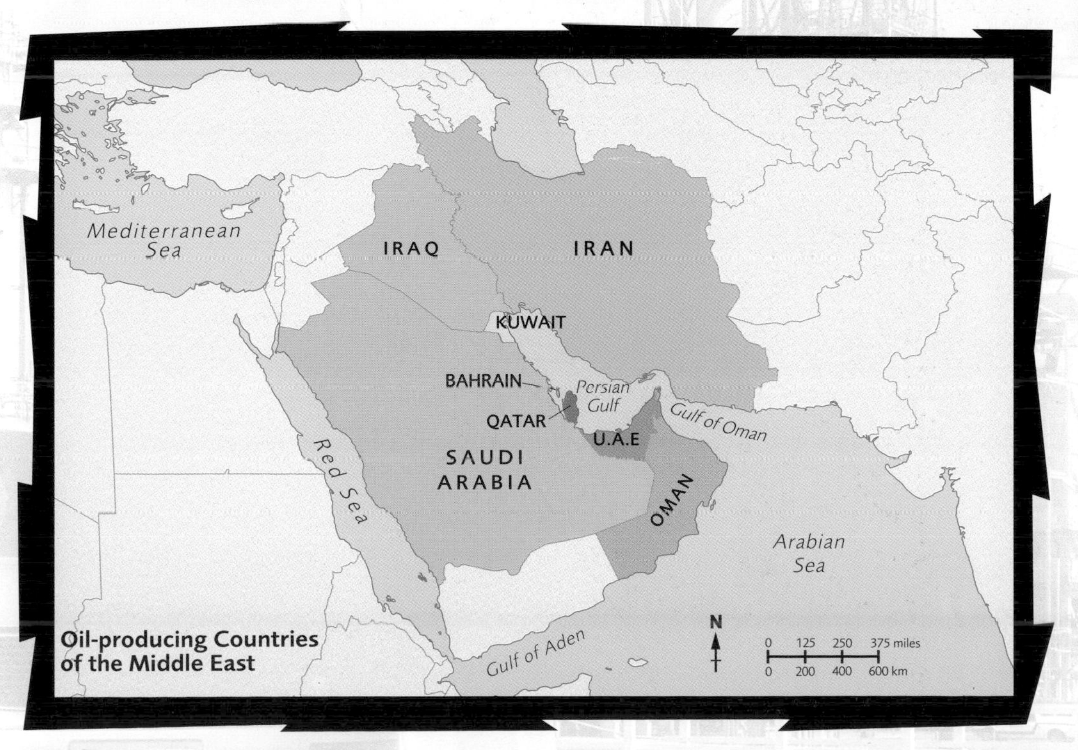

The Middle East Before Oil

Before oil was discovered there in the 20th century, most people in the West had barely heard of the Middle East. Those who had heard of the region knew it mainly as the ancient birthplace of many of the world's civilizations and religions.

Most people who lived in the Middle East were poor, working at farming, herding animals or trading. Some lived a nomadic lifestyle, moving from place to place with their herds of animals, setting up camps in the desert as they had for centuries.

The greatest power in the Middle East was the Turkish **Ottoman Empire**, which had its capital in Istanbul. Most of the Arabic-speaking countries we know today were parts of the Ottoman Empire. They did not yet exist as independent states. Only Iran was a separate country, with its own language, **Persian**.

Baghdad in 1917: Sunni Arabs and Jews rubbed shoulders with northern Kurds, **Shi'ites** from the south, Turks and Persians.

Labourers dig a trench during the construction of the Suez Canal in Egypt in 1860. The canal linked the Red Sea to the Mediterranean, cutting the time for European ships to reach India and China. This made the Middle East important to countries such as Great Britain and France, which had business interests in the Far East.

"It is a principle of British policy that we cannot allow any rival political interest in the waters of the Gulf."
(Lord Curzon, the British governor of India, explains in 1911 that Britain will not let another country gain power in the Persian Gulf. Britain wanted to keep control of shipping routes to India.)

Powerful European governments did have some interest in the Middle East. France had links with Christian communities in the areas which later became Syria and Lebanon. Great Britain traded in Iraq and the Gulf states. Later, the Suez Canal in Egypt became important to both Britain and France. The canal provided a short sea route to the Far East, allowing goods to travel to and from European territories in India, China and French Indochina much more quickly than before.

Most of the **Arabian Peninsula** (the area where much of the Middle East's oil is found today) was barren desert. Arabia was still very important to Muslims around the world, however, because of the holy cities of Mecca and Medina.

The First Middle East Oil Discoveries

> **“The Allies in World War I floated to victory on a sea of oil.”**
> *(Lord Curzon, British statesman and Viceroy of India, 1911)*

The transformation of the Middle East began when oil was discovered there. In the early 20th century in Europe and the USA, industry and transport increasingly relied on oil as a source of power. More and more oil was needed every year. Soon, much of it would be coming from the Middle East.

The first Middle Eastern oil was found in Persia, the country now known as Iran. The ruler of Persia, the Shah, first allowed oil exploration in 1901. Both American and British companies worked in Persia.

In 1914, just as World War I was about to begin, the British government bought a majority of the **shares** in the Anglo-Persian Oil Company. It did this because the British navy's ships now ran on oil. The British hoped to make sure they would always have a source of fuel for their navy. Oil would prove to be an important resource in World War I.

These workers are drilling for oil in Persia in 1909. The tower above the drill is called a 'derrick'.

The next Middle Eastern country in which oil was discovered was Iraq, where exploration began before World War I. Great Britain took political control of Iraq after the war, when the **League of Nations** asked it to govern Iraq under a special arrangement called a **mandate**. The world's most powerful countries all wanted to gain control of Iraq's oil. In 1925 the government of Iraq signed an agreement giving the Iraq Petroleum Company permission to explore for oil. The Iraq Petroleum Company was owned by British, Dutch, French and US interests.

When oil exploration began in Saudi Arabia, American companies gained control of the oil industry. In 1933 the Standard Oil Company of California signed an agreement with King Ibn Saud of Saudi Arabia. The first commercial oilfield was discovered in Dammam, Saudi Arabia, in 1938 (see pages 16–17).

'OIL'!

'At four o'clock in the morning, there was a tremendous noise of shouting and scuffling. The dramatic scene put an end to sleep. Spouting high over the top of the derrick, [18 to 24 metres] into the morning air, was a black fountain of oil'. (A witness describes the discovery of oil in Saudi Arabia in 1938)

"We recognize in the Persian oilfield a necessary source of supply for a long period of time. Is it not wiser to gain control of it?"
(Winston Churchill, 17 June 1914)

Winston Churchill in 1914, just before World War I. Churchill bought shares in the Anglo-Persian Oil Company for the British navy to ensure that Britain's ships had oil for the war.

The Spread of the Oil Industry

Iraq was the second Middle Eastern country in which oil was discovered. For a time, Iraq became the Middle East's most important oil producer.

After World War I, Great Britain controlled the territory that was to become Iraq. The British authorities were determined that the potentially oil-rich northern province of Mosul, occupied by British troops in 1918, should become part of the new country. In 1925 Mosul did become part of the new Iraqi state, and in 1927 the oil prospectors finally got their reward: they found oil at Baba Gurgur in northern Iraq. The **gusher** at Baba Gurgur was even more spectacular than the oil strikes in Persia had been, shooting oil 80 metres (260 feet) into the air for weeks until it was brought under control.

Iraq looked set to become a major oil producer. Britain granted Iraq independence in 1932, but did not completely give up control. An agreement allowed Britain to keep troops in Iraq, and Britain claimed the right to cancel laws made by the new government. By 1939 Iraq still produced only 2 per cent of the world's oil. However, this was destined to grow rapidly.

14 October 1927: a day of destiny in Iraq. Oil gushes uncontrollably at Baba Gurgur in northern Iraq, where the Turkish Petroleum Company's driller struck oil.

> **"Oil appears in the desert and can't be exploited by the Arabs, and the British and American oil companies are very aggressive. Someone is going to develop this oil..."**
> *(A comment by J. S. Mann, a British official in Iraq in 1920)*

Celebrations in 1952 on the completion of a 895-kilometre (556-mile) pipeline from northern Iraq to the Mediterranean coast of Syria.

Around the world, especially after the end of World War II, other oil consumers were also beginning to recognize the importance of Middle Eastern oil. European countries in particular knew that they were going to need more oil than could be bought from the USA. The rapid growth of US industry meant that most of the USA's oil was used inside the country, with little left over for sale abroad.

'MR 5 PER CENT'

When one of the new oil companies, the Turkish Petroleum Company, was set up, 5 per cent was reserved for a Turkish Armenian businessman named Calouste Gulbenkian. Gulbenkian had played a part in many oil deals in Iraq, going back to the days of the Ottoman Empire. 'Mr 5 Per cent', as Gulbenkian came to be known, became one of the richest men in the world on the proceeds.

Oil in the Gulf States

In the early 20th century, the hunt was also on for oil in the Gulf sheikhdoms. These were the small countries on the eastern coast of Arabia which were controlled by Great Britain.

Britain had been trading with Basra, a city in what is now Iraq, since the mid-19th century. Problems in the Gulf might have affected Britain's trade, so the British soon began to take control of the region's governments. In 1880 Bahrain became a British **protectorate**, which meant that British troops could be stationed there. Kuwait became a protectorate in 1899. Qatar, Oman and other Gulf states soon also came under British control.

Ibn Saud, the future King of Saudi Arabia, meets British officials during World War I. In the centre of the picture is Sir Percy Cox, who drew up the borders of Iraq and Kuwait.

OIL PRODUCTION FIGURES, 1939

WORLD:
USA: 1.28 billion barrels (60 per cent of world production)
Soviet Union: 221 million barrels (10 per cent of world production)

MIDDLE EAST:
Iran: 78 million barrels (3.6 per cent of world production)
Iraq: 31 million barrels (1.5 per cent of world production)
Saudi Arabia: 4 million barrels (0.2 per cent of world production)

"If there seems any hope of obtaining oil, we shall never give a **concession** [allowance] in this matter to anyone except a person appointed by the British government."
(Sheikh Mubarak Al-Sabah of Kuwait writing to British officials in 1913)

Abdul Aziz Ibn Abdul Rahman Al Saud, known as Ibn Saud, pictured in 1911. Ibn Saud later became the first King of Saudi Arabia.

The only territory the British did not control was the area that became Saudi Arabia. In 1915 Britain signed a treaty with the Saudi ruler, Ibn Saud. The British agreed that Ibn Saud was ruler of the eastern and central parts of Arabia. In exchange, he agreed that he would not try to control Kuwait, Bahrain, Qatar, the small sheikhdoms that later became the United Arab Emirates and Oman. These areas, and their oilfields, were still controlled by the British.

After World War I, Britain set out the borders between all the states of the Arabian Peninsula. British 'advisers', backed up by troops, made sure that the rulers of the small Gulf states followed the British government's wishes.

The oilfields in Bahrain, Kuwait and Qatar were developed mainly by British-controlled oil companies. In Bahrain the first oil was produced in 1933, and enough was flowing by 1937 to be worth **exporting** for sale. In Kuwait and Qatar, drilling began before World War II, though oil only began to be sold abroad once the war had finished.

Arabian Explorations

By the 1930s, the UK controlled many of the smaller oil-producing Gulf states. But in Saudi Arabia, the largest Gulf country, the USA took control of the oil business.

The first agreement to take oil from Saudi Arabia's oilfields was given to an American oil company in 1933. Standard Oil of California, later known as Chevron, paid the Saudi Arabian government for the right to explore for oil. Many other countries attempted to gain a foothold in Saudi Arabia, but the King preferred to do business with the Americans, who offered him the best deals.

Workers drill a well in the Qatif oilfield, Saudi Arabia, in the early 1940s.

King Ibn Saud was an impressive figure, but he had no training as a businessman. So he was very pleased that the American oil companies were promising to pay him what seemed like vast sums of money, if they succeeded in finding oil.

> **"Put your trust in God, and sign."**
> *(Ibn Saud, instructing his chief minister to allow prospecting for oil. The king hoped that oil would bring riches to Saudi Arabia.)*

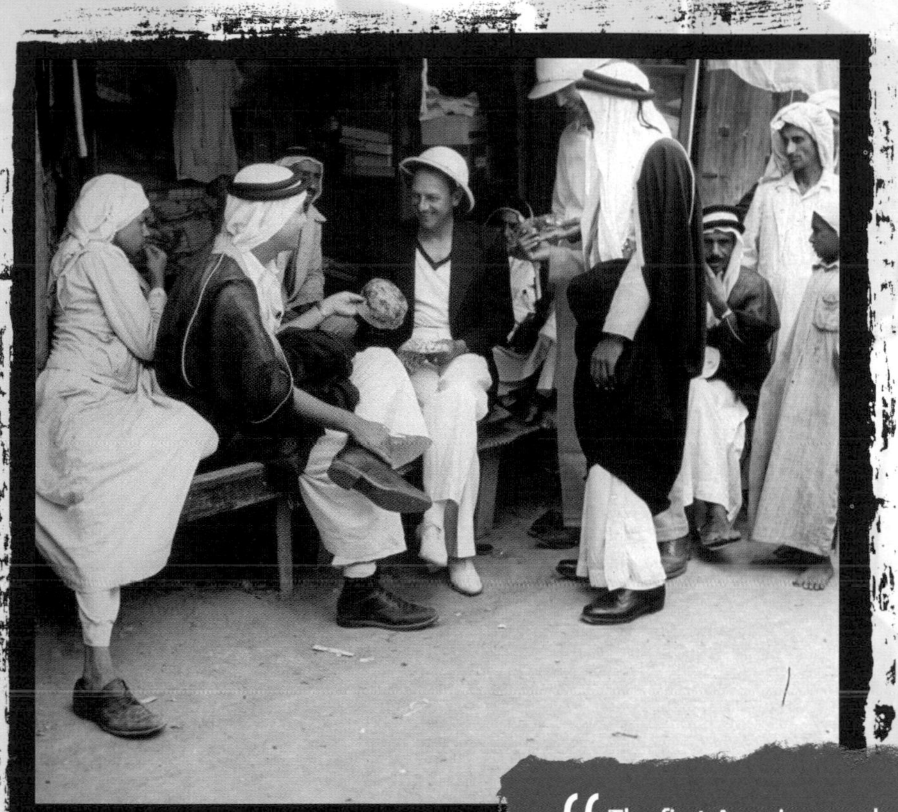

Friendly Saudis offer the oil explorers gifts.

Oil was not discovered straight away. Even though geologists knew the type of land where oil was often found, there were rarely visible signs that it was there. The only clue was sometimes a black deposit called bitumen, which told them where to drill into the ground. The explorers lived alongside desert tribes called Bedouin. They avoided the **Wahhabi** Muslims, who hated the presence of non-Muslim foreigners.

In 1938, when the first oil discovery was finally made, US personnel flooded into Saudi Arabia. Wells, pipelines and oil storage tanks sprang up in the desert. Local people also began to work in the oil industry. In May 1939 the first oil tanker loaded its cargo.

"The first American explorers in eastern Arabia dressed themselves in Arab clothes, grew thick beards and had a dozen of Ibn Saud's colourful soldiers as guides and protectors while they mapped and trekked the desert for hundreds of miles. They were often cut off for weeks on end."

(Wayne Mineau, an American oil explorer, describes his experiences in Saudi Arabia before World War II)

Oil in World War II

Oil was a crucial factor in World War II, but little Middle Eastern oil was used, except that from Iran. The **Allies** were careful to keep the war away from the oil states. Oil from the USA, Mexico and Venezuela kept the wheels of the Allied armies turning.

"For the purpose of lend-lease aid to Saudi Arabia, I hereby find that the defence of Saudi Arabia is vital to the defence of the United States."

(US President Roosevelt in 1943)

Germany and the countries on its side, who made up the **Axis powers**, were in a more difficult position. Middle Eastern oil was a target for the Axis powers, which had little oil except for some sources in Central European countries such as Romania and Hungary.

British armoured cars arrive in Iran during World War II. They were there to protect the British-owned oil industry in Abadan.

Oil production in Iran continued throughout the war, but did not increase. Iraq also continued to produce oil. In 1941 an attempted **military coup** by a group of Iraqis sympathetic to Germany, which could have handed Iraq's oil to the Axis powers, was quickly crushed by British troops. Finally, German efforts to reach the oilfields of the Middle East from Egypt were stopped by Allied victory in North Africa.

In the Gulf, the oil business almost came to a halt during the war. There was no money for new exploration, and oil production was limited. The Saudi government found itself short of money.

The USA government decided to give aid to Saudi Arabia. American help, some of which was called 'lend-lease', included cash payments made in silver. Some of the silver was even made into the Saudi currency, the riyal, before it left the USA. This allowed Ibn Saud to pay his debts and keep his kingdom going.

BRITISH-AMERICAN RIVALRY

In 1941 Ibn Saud was running out of money. He turned to the British for help. The UK offered Saudi Arabia food and money, and seemed to be attempting to build a relationship with Saudi Arabia to rival that of the USA. This was one reason for the US aid, and for the US decision after World War II to make the links between the USA and Saudi Arabia as close as possible.

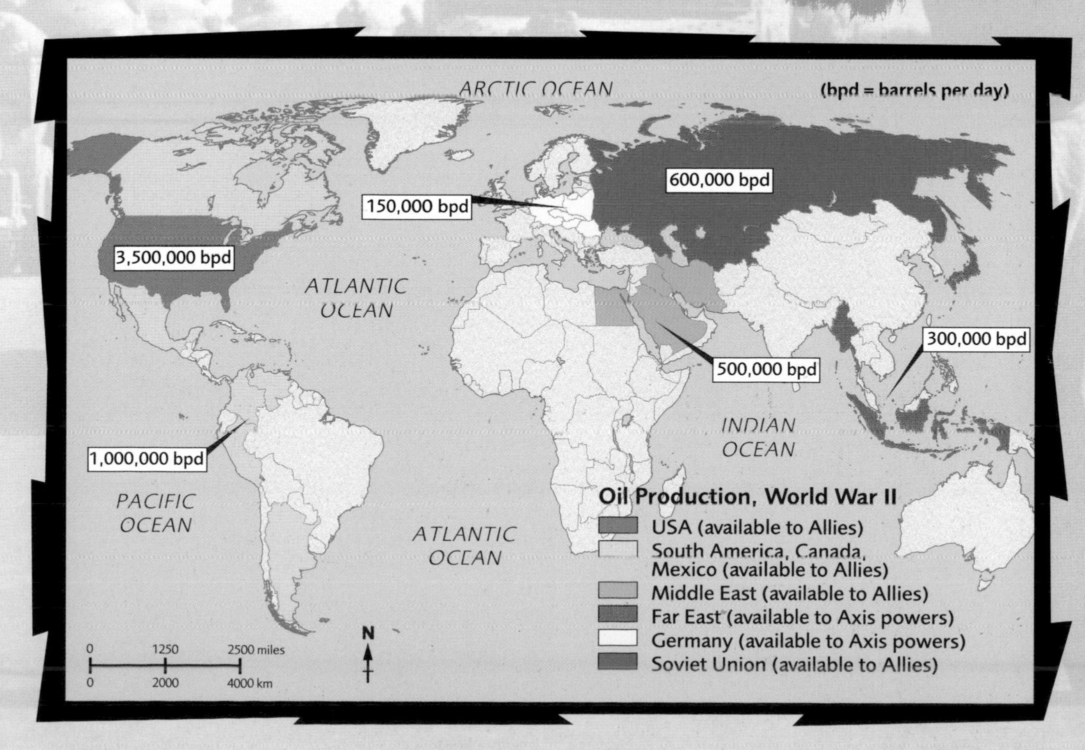

During World War II, access to oil was vital. Without oil, factories could not make weapons and armed forces could not continue to fight.

The USA and Saudi Arabia

At the end of World War II, the USA could see that Saudi Arabia would be a vital source of oil stretching far into the future. The US government and oil companies decided to build close links with Saudi Arabia.

In 1944 the US oil companies operating in Saudi Arabia set up a new company, Aramco. They hoped that Aramco would be able to make the Saudi Arabian oil business grow quickly, turning Saudi Arabia into a wealthy country, and making the oil companies rich at the same time!

The US government also wanted to build a close relationship with Saudi Arabia, where much of the world's future oil supply might well be located. In February 1945 President Franklin D. Roosevelt met Ibn Saud on the *USS Quincy*, which was moored in Egypt's Suez Canal. Roosevelt was by then very sick, but was still determined to meet with King Saud.

"First, you are good oil men, second, you treat your Arab employees as equals, third, you are a big and powerful country, but more interested in business than politics. And fourth, you are a long way away!"
(Ibn Saud explaining why he trusted the Americans)

King Ibn Saud and President Franklin D. Roosevelt on the deck of the *USS Quincy* on 20 February 1945.

During their meeting, Ibn Saud spoke mostly of the fate of **Palestine**, where it was rumoured that the Western Allies planned to create a Jewish state. As an Arab Muslim, Ibn Saud wanted Palestine to remain Muslim, rather than be controlled by non-Arab Jewish people.

The two leaders had some things in common. Each said he was at heart a simple farmer. Both men were disabled and unable to walk, and Roosevelt presented one of his wheelchairs to Ibn Saud as a gift. Apparently Ibn Saud was reassured that he could trust the USA.

IBN SAUD AND FDR

An interpreter named William Eddy summed up the meeting between Ibn Saud and President Roosevelt: 'In very simple language, Ibn Saud asked FDR for his friendship. The president then gave Ibn Saud two assurances: 1) he personally, as president, would never do anything which might prove hostile to the Arabs; 2) the US government would make no change in its basic policy in Palestine without full consultation with both Jews and Arabs.'

This picture shows Aramco's large oil installations at the Saudi port of Dahran in 1945, seen from the air.

Post-war Boom and Disruption

After the end of World War II, the oil industry in the Middle East began to grow rapidly. By 1949 oil production there was mostly under the control of seven major international oil companies, known in the industry as the Seven Sisters.

For a while, nothing seemed to slow the growth of the oil industry. However, there were problems on the horizon. The governments of the USA and Europe were about to become very unpopular with many of the Middle East's people. The creation in 1948 of a Jewish country, Israel, created an angry atmosphere. Most of the Middle East's people were Muslims. They hated the idea of having a Jewish country as a neighbour, on land which they thought was Muslim land. To make matters worse for the Arabs, the Western countries that bought most of their oil (the USA and the UK) were the very ones which had helped set up Israel.

"Oil proved to be the most important consideration in America's Middle Eastern policy. The United States sought to balance support for the new state of Israel against the pressures of the oil producers, mostly Arab."
(*The Houghton Mifflin* Reader's Companion to American History)

Young Arabs in particular became hostile to Arab governments they thought were too close to the West. In Iraq, for example, a military coup overthrew the monarchy in 1958. The king and the prime minister were killed. In the years that followed, the Iraq Petroleum Company was taken over by the new Iraqi government.

Iran's Prime Minister Dr Mohammed Mossadegh (right) shakes hands with a British official in 1951.

Iranians in Tehran demonstrate in favour of the Iranian government's plan to nationalize the Anglo-Iranian Oil Company in 1951.

In Iran there were troubles that the West was able to overcome. In 1951 the **nationalist** prime minister, Dr Mossadegh, demanded that the oil industry be **nationalized**. The Anglo-Iranian Oil Company became the National Iranian Oil Company. But in 1953 Dr Mossadegh was overthrown, apparently with the help of the **CIA** and British intelligence. The pro-Western Shah once more took control, and the West regained its influence over the oil industry.

Only in the Gulf was there little change in the West's relationship with the Middle East oil producers. Even here, however, the hatred with which the Arabs viewed Israel created difficulties between their governments and the West.

'THE MAJORS'

The oil companies known in the 1950s as the Seven Sisters, also called the 'majors', were:

- **US companies Esso, Mobil, Standard Oil of California, Gulf and Texaco**
- **BP (British Petroleum)**
- **Shell (a British-Dutch company).**

The Seven Sisters owned the companies that worked the oilfields in each region. The French company CFP was the only other big oil company.

OPEC

OPEC is short for the Organization of Petroleum Exporting Countries. OPEC was founded in 1960, and plays a crucial role in the Middle East oil industry. OPEC's main job is to help the oil-producing countries set the worldwide price of oil.

The first move towards the creation of OPEC was a meeting of Arab oil producers in Cairo in 1959, known as the First Arab Petroleum Congress. Representatives of two non-Arab countries also came to the meeting. One of these was Iran, which was also in the Middle East, and the other was Venezuela. Venezuela was the major oil producer in South America, and was eager to help set up an oil producers' body. In 1960 Saudi Arabia, Iraq, Kuwait, Iran and Venezuela together founded OPEC.

Why were the oil producers so keen to set up their own organization? The reason was that until the 1960s, it was the oil companies which told producing countries how much they would pay for the oil they extracted. This system was known as '**posted prices**'. Around this time these prices were quite low.

After its formation, OPEC began to demand a higher price for oil, and a bigger percentage of the money the companies made from the oil.

> **"OPEC [was] a direct reaction to a reduction in the 'posted price' of crude oil in the Persian Gulf. The price cuts of August 1960 were the last the companies were ever able to make."**
> (*J. E. Hartshorn*, Politics and World Oil Economics)

Delegates from Saudi Arabia, Libya and Kuwait (from left to right) at an OPEC meeting in 1968.

An oil worker monitors operations on an off-shore rig in the Gulf in 1970.

In 1971, at a meeting in Tehran, Iran, OPEC tried to set higher prices for oil for the first time. OPEC's attempts to set oil prices were not always successful. A **free market** in non-OPEC oil began to develop, which tended to stop prices rising too high.

Today, OPEC countries produce less than 40 per cent of the world's oil, so it cannot completely control prices. However, OPEC's influence may increase as oil begins to run out, which might mean OPEC's share of world production increases.

OPEC MEMBERS, 2005

Founder Members: Iraq, Kuwait, Saudi Arabia, Iran, Venezuela.

Arab states: Algeria, Iraq, Kuwait, Libya, Qatar, Saudi Arabia, UAE.

Non-Arab states: Venezuela, Indonesia, Iran, Nigeria, Ecuador, Gabon.

The Oil Shock of 1973

In 1973 Egypt launched a surprise attack on Israeli forces occupying the Egyptian Sinai peninsula. War broke out between Israel and the Arabs. For the first time, oil was used as a political weapon.

In 1968 the Arabs had come together to form another international oil producers' organization called OAPEC, the Organization of Arab Petroleum Exporting Countries. In October 1973, after the outbreak of war, OAPEC announced it would cut production and ban oil exports to the USA. The Arabs knew that the West depended on their oil. They hoped that increasing the price of oil would force Western governments to persuade Israel to agree to Arab political demands.

The West's reaction was hostile, but it could do nothing. The system of 'posted prices' set by the oil companies had ended years before. The Western oil-consuming countries referred to what happened as the 'oil shock' of 1973.

"After 1960 the oil producing countries were finally able to break the chains of servitude [slavery] to the major oil companies."
(*Abdulaziz al-Sowayegh*, Arab Petro-politics)

8 October 1973: OPEC meets at its Vienna, Austria headquarters after the outbreak of the Arab war with Israel.

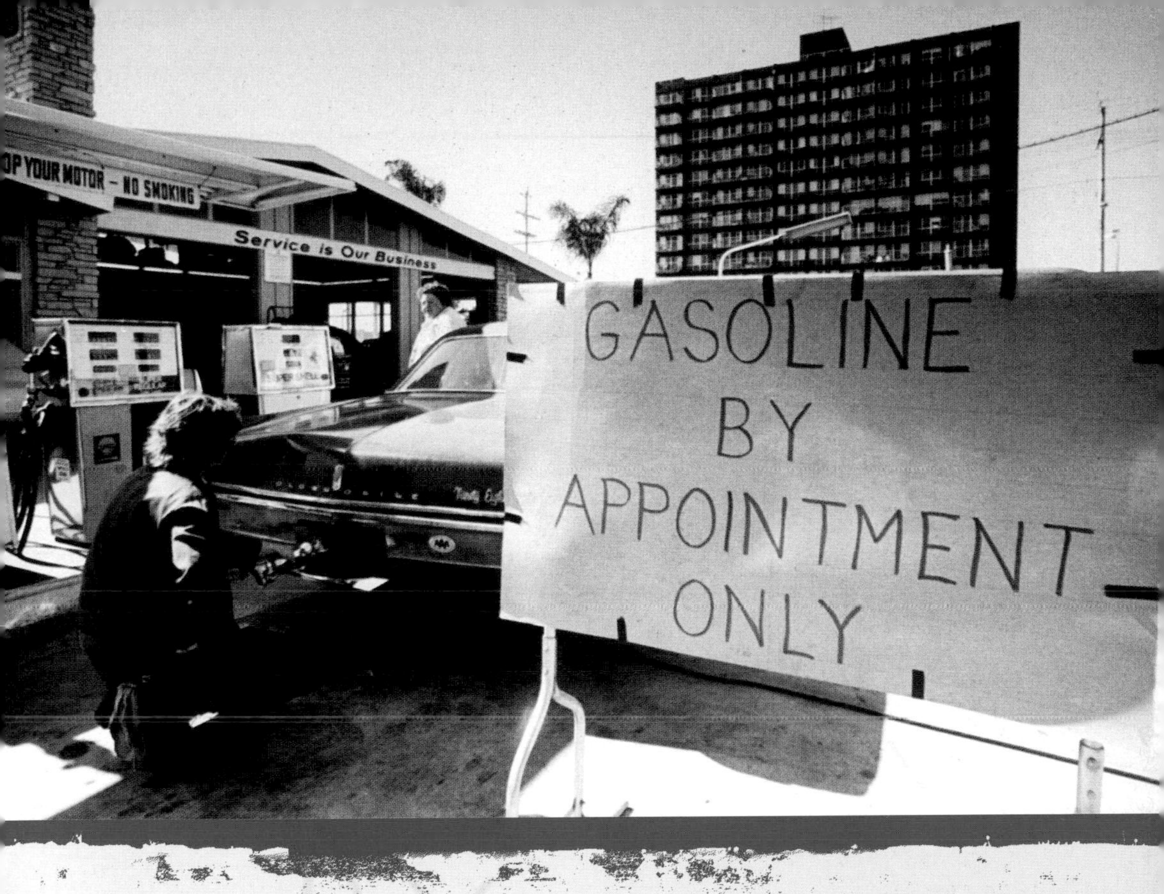

The effects of the oil shock were felt across the USA in 1974.

At the height of the oil shock, oil prices increased by four times in a year. There were long queues at petrol stations, and cars regularly ground to a stop at the side of the road, having run out of petrol. Industry was affected too, as energy for factories and machines became more expensive. The USA had to buy oil from non-OAPEC sources, which became very expensive.

After the oil shock, prices did slowly go down again. But they would never again fall to the levels of the days when the companies had set prices. Oil would remain more expensive than before, and over the years its price would steadily increase.

The oil shock caused the West to buy more of its oil from non-Middle Eastern sources. In 1982 OPEC decided on a policy of setting **production quotas**, which told each member country how much oil it should produce. Cutting the amount produced raised the price of oil, and increasing the amount produced lowered the price. Not all countries always did as they were told, but generally, the system meant that the oil-producing countries were able to control the world price of oil.

Oil and Political Change

In the 1970s there was another big change for the oil industry in the Middle East, as the oil-producing countries became the owners of the oil companies.

In 1973 Iraq nationalized (took over ownership of) the remaining foreign oil companies operating within its borders. Kuwait had also nationalized its oil industry by 1975, and in 1976 Saudi Arabia bought 100 per cent of Aramco. In these countries, foreigners worked as contractors but the state was the owner. After the Islamic Revolution in Iran in 1979, the Iranian oil industry was also gradually brought under government control. World oil prices soon shot upwards. This was because people feared that the flow of oil might be interrupted by the Revolution. In fact the government of Iran kept the oil flowing because it badly needed the income from oil. Iran used its oil income for development. It built new schools, hospitals, roads and other facilities for its people.

Iran's neighbour, Iraq, also funded development using money from oil sales. Iran and Iraq fought a war against each other between 1980 and 1988. This long war between two oil states cost each of them dearly, and set back the modernization and development of both countries.

This burning oil tanker was hit by an Iranian missile in December 1987, during the Iran-Iraq war.

> **“In the 1970s, nationalization … became the major issue between the Western countries that were home to the oil companies and the producing countries. By 1976 complete nationalization [had happened].”**
> *(Benjamin Shwadran,* **Middle East Oil***)*

The rulers of Saudi Arabia and the Gulf states meet in the 1970s to discuss oil policy.

In the Gulf the money flowed more directly towards the personal pockets of the rulers. In Saudi Arabia and the small Gulf states, the oil money went mostly to the rulers. However, some countries, such as Kuwait, Qatar and Abu Dhabi (in the United Arab Emirates), set up organizations for investing in non-petroleum related industries. They were planning for the day when the oil ran out, and they had no more to sell.

Some oil profit in the Gulf does benefit the ordinary people. In Saudi Arabia and the Gulf states, there is no income tax. The government pays most of the costs of healthcare and education. In addition, however, all the Gulf states, including Saudi Arabia, have used much of their oil money to buy arms.

THE UK AND THE GULF

After World War II, the UK withdrew from the Gulf countries that it had previously controlled. Oman became independent in 1951, and Kuwait in 1961. Bahrain, Qatar and the smaller sheikhdoms became independent in 1971. The smaller states grouped themselves together into a single federal state, called the United Arab Emirates.

Oil and Society

Oil has had a huge impact on the people and society of each of the Middle Eastern oil states. Although oil created riches for some, others still live in real poverty.

The personal wealth of the rulers of Saudi Arabia comes from oil, and is immense. The Gulf ruling families are also vastly wealthy, but not on the same scale as the Saudis. King Fahd of Saudi Arabia was said to have owned palaces that he had never even seen. At the same time, there were still poor people living in his country.

In Saudi Arabia and the Gulf there is also an emerging group of people who are neither fabulously rich nor poor. Their money has come directly or indirectly from oil, but they are not members of the ruling families. Many have been educated abroad. Such people own and run many businesses in the Gulf and Saudi Arabia. However, most ordinary Saudis have not been made wealthy by oil, though they benefit from the medical services and education the Kingdom provides.

Tradition in the United Arab Emirates sheikhdom of Abu Dhabi. This man is practising the traditional sport of falconry.

"In the Gulf, the old ways are dying out, the memories are dimming, the old men who knew it all are disappearing."
(John Bullock, in his book **The Gulf**, *explains how life in the Gulf is changing)*

An immigrant construction worker from India helps to build a new skyscraper in Jeddah, Saudi Arabia.

In the other oil-producing countries, such as Iran and Iraq, oil money has gone to the government, and has not created such great personal wealth as in the Gulf. In these countries, oil money has helped raise the standard of living of ordinary people. In Iraq, for example, before the catastrophe of Saddam Hussein's wars (see pages 32–35), the standard of living had risen to that of a European country such as Greece.

In Iran, with a large population of almost 70 million, the money has been more thinly spread. Before his overthrow in 1979, the Shah of Iran used oil money to build up Iran's industries (though people also said he spent much of Iran's money on weapons and personal luxuries). Since 1979 the Islamic Republic has also used some of the profits from oil to try and improve life for ordinary Iranians.

IMMIGRANT WORKERS

Much of the work in Saudi Arabia is done by an army of immigrants. These immigrants do everything from administration to manual labour. Engineers and computer specialists may come from the West, while accountants and managers come from other Arab countries, India and Pakistan. Many workers are brought in from Bangladesh, and domestic servants, truck drivers, nurses and doctors often come from the Philippines.

Saddam Hussein and Iraq

Iraq's former president Saddam Hussein shoulders an RPG (Rocket-Propelled Grenade Launcher) during the Iran-Iraq war of 1980–1988.

In 1979 Saddam Hussein became president of Iraq. No one knew it at the time, but the stage was set for more than two decades of conflict. Iraq was to fight wars with its neighbours, then with countries from elsewhere in the world. Saddam aimed to become the Middle East's most powerful ruler.

Saddam Hussein was the leader of Iraq's **Ba'ath Party**. The word *ba'ath* means 'renaissance' or 'rebirth', and the aims of the Party were to turn the Arab people into a nation. The Ba'ath Party wanted to unite the Arabs, making them stronger and providing them with a better standard of living. Saddam Hussein's version of Ba'athism, however, was a dictatorship with him in charge.

By the time Saddam became the leader of Iraq, the oil industry there was completely controlled by the Iraqi Oil Ministry. Saddam used the revenue from Iraq's oil to buy weapons and form an army to fight his wars. It also provided him and his supporters with a luxurious lifestyle.

"Our people in Khuzestan [the Iraqi name for part of Iran] should prepare themselves to exercise legitimate national rights over their territories and to play their part as a people worthy to become a nation."
(Saddam Hussein, speaking on 14 March 1981)

Within Iraq, Saddam Hussein took complete control. His secret police arrested and tortured his opponents. Outside Iraq, Saddam feared attacks from his neighbours, but he also wanted to dominate the region.

US warships escort Kuwaiti oil tankers through the Gulf in 1987, during the Iran-Iraq War.

From 1980 to 1988, Iraq was at war with Iran. What were the causes of this war?

- Saddam Hussein feared Iran, where the Islamic Republic had been declared in 1979. He was worried that the Shi'ite Islamic Revolution could spread into Iraq, where most people were also Shi'ites.
- Saddam thought Iran wanted to gain control of the Shatt el-Arab, the waterway that separates the two countries. The Shatt-el-Arab is a major sea lane for oil tankers.
- Saddam wanted to gain control of south-west Iran, known in Iraq as Khuzestan. This was where Iran's oil wealth was located. Many of the people there were Arabs, not Persians.

THE GULF AND IRAN

The oil-rich states of the Gulf supported Iraq with loans and other favours during its war with Iran. The Gulf states feared attack by the Islamic Republic of Iran. They hoped Saddam Hussein could keep away the threat from non-Arab Iran and militant Islam.

The eight-year conflict left over a million dead with no gains or losses of territory. By the end of the war, Iraq's oil production had fallen. Saddam had spent huge amounts of money on weapons. He owed billions of dollars to Kuwait. In 1990 Saddam decided to attack Kuwait. He aimed to cancel the debt to Kuwait and capture its oil wells. In fact, Saddam's forces were quickly defeated by a US-led coalition (see pages 4–5). The Iraqis were chased from Kuwait, and Saddam's position worsened, because he was no longer allowed to use the revenue from oil to buy weapons.

Iraq and Oil Today

During the twelve years after Iraq's invasion of Kuwait, Iraq was subject to United Nations sanctions. In 1996 the United Nations brought in an Oil-for-Food Programme. Iraq was allowed to export oil to buy food and medicine. This gave the country an income and kept the oil industry running, but the average Iraqi saw little benefit. Malnutrition increased, medicines were scarce and only the military and those close to Saddam seemed to prosper.

The United Nations set up inspection schemes to make sure that Iraq was getting rid of weapons it was no longer allowed to have, including its **weapons of mass destruction** (WMD). Various schemes failed to prove that these weapons had been destroyed. This was partly because the Iraqi government would not cooperate with the weapons inspectors. The USA and other countries, mainly the UK, decided that military action against Iraq was necessary to destroy Iraq's WMDs. The invasion of Iraq took place in March 2003.

Members of the United Nations inspection team examine sites for evidence of banned weapons of mass destruction in Iraq in December 2002. No such arms were ever found.

A US soldier helps guard an oil refinery at Kissik, Iraq, in October 2003.

> **"A simple attack produces a huge impact. It's cheap, easy to do, and achievable."**
> *(Mustafa Alani, oil consultant)*

Iraq threatened to destroy its own oil installations, but in the end it did not do so. Nonetheless, oil production was stopped temporarily. The military administration put in place by the Allies, known as the **Coalition Provisional Authority**, succeeded in restarting the flow of oil. However, production remained lower than in 1991, and attacks by Iraqi **insurgent** fighters caused regular interruptions.

Iraq's oil remained under the control of Iraq's own oil ministry, part of the **Interim** Iraqi Government which was formed in June 2004. Even so, some people claimed that one of the true reasons for the invasion was that the Allies, and in particular the USA, wanted to gain control over Iraq's oil industry. Cash from the export of oil helped to pay the costs of reconstruction and the US-led occupation. Iraqi oil exports suffered after attacks by insurgents. And because Iraq's oil refineries were not working at full speed, some petrol for local use had to be imported.

IRAQI OIL UNDER ATTACK

After sovereignty was handed over to Iraq's Interim Government in June 2004, attacks by insurgents on Iraq's oilfields and pipelines increased. By early 2005, there were up to a dozen attacks a day. Iraq has 6,000 kilometres (3,700 miles) of pipelines, which are virtually impossible to protect.

Islamic Iran

In 1979 Iran was transformed by the overthrow of the Shah. The exiled religious leader, the Ayatollah Khomeini, returned to take charge of the new Islamic Republic of Iran. Oil, though, continued to be the backbone of Iran's economy.

Iran underwent a complete transformation in 1979, but it still needed income from oil to survive. Developed countries were as willing to buy from the Islamic Republic as they had been from the Shah. In general, the country's new Islamic rulers were eager to continue just one of the Shah's old policies: industrial development using money from oil sales.

Ayatollah Khomeini, the leader of the Islamic Revolution, greets his supporters soon after his return to Iran in 1979.

There were some changes after the Revolution. The National Iranian Oil Company (NIOC), a state body that had existed under the Shah, had been developing and exploiting oil resources alongside the foreign oil companies. Under the Islamic Republic, an oil ministry was formed to oversee the oil industry. The NIOC, which was Iran's own oil corporation, took complete control of the Iranian oil industry.

The war between Iran and Iraq from 1980 to 1988 used up many of the resources available to both sides. The war slowed down and damaged the oil industries in both countries. A strange situation was created. Both countries were members of OPEC, but they were at war. They certainly didn't want to sit down together at OPEC's headquarters in Vienna, Austria to make decisions on price policy and quotas.

However, both Iran and Iraq continued to be bound by OPEC's prices, though not without difficulties. At different times during the war, both countries ignored OPEC's line on prices and production.

“When we look at Iran, we see a danger for the West. It is the foremost sponsor of state terrorism and assassination across the globe. We wish to encourage a change in Iranian behaviour.”

(The US State Department, 1993)

GUEST COMPANIES

Article 43 of the Constitution of the Islamic Republic of Iran banned foreigners from dominating Iran's economy. But in 1987 a special law for the oil ministry allowed contracts between the state and foreign oil companies. A 'guest company' working in Iran could be rewarded by allowing it to export a certain amount of oil for its own profit.

In March 1995, however, US President Bill Clinton signed a law banning American companies from working in the Iranian oil industry, mainly because of Iran's record on human rights and terrorism.

Iran in the 21st Century

A huge mural of Ayatollah Khomeini looks out on streets packed with cars during the evening rush hour in Iran's capital, Tehran.

Iran continues to be one of the world's major oil states and an active member of OPEC. But as the 21st century began, US President George W. Bush said that Iran was part of what he called an 'Axis of Evil'. This caused some people to think that the USA could be planning to lead an attack on Iran like the one it had led on Iraq.

The Axis of Evil identified by George W. Bush is made up of states that the USA says support terrorism and are hostile to the West. However, Iran continued to export its oil to Europe and elsewhere, in spite of sanctions that were imposed by the USA.

Some European countries said at the time that continuing to trade with Iran and allowing it to export its oil helped the reformers inside Iran – those who favoured more friendly relations with the West. The USA took a tougher line, believing that Iran should be isolated until it fell in line with Western ideas. Islamic Iran, for its part, does not want to be an isolated country, and wants foreign investment in its oil industry.

There is a special reason why the USA has maintained a tough line on Iran in the early years of the 21st century. This is because of Iran's policy of developing nuclear power. Iran is alone among the oil states in having a large population. Iran claims it is developing nuclear technology in order to use nuclear power for its domestic needs, while reserving its oil for export. In this way it can sell its oil for hard currency, in order to buy necessary imports for future development. However, evidence suggests that Iran could also be trying to develop nuclear weapons.

WEAPONS OR FUEL?

The USA believes that Iran is trying to produce nuclear weapons. It claims that Iran has been refining raw uranium, the material that fuels nuclear power stations, to the level where it could be used for nuclear weapons. Iran on the other hand claims it is only making its own nuclear fuel, which international agreements allow.

Nuclear technicians work to install a nuclear reactor inside Iran's nuclear power plant at Bushehr.

"It is not acceptable that developed countries generate 70 or 80 per cent of their electricity from nuclear energy and tell Iran, a great and powerful nation, that it cannot have nuclear electricity. Iran does not accept this."

(Ali Akbar Rafsanjani, former president of Iran)

The Gulf and Oil Today

By the 1980s the Gulf states were all independent countries. All were governed by monarchs. The biggest problem they faced was that their increasingly wealthy and educated people wanted more say in how they were governed. Some Gulf rulers have been attempting to introduce an element of democracy into their countries.

The Gulf states are all producers of oil and natural gas, though some have more oil than others. These oil resources will probably last for many decades, and perhaps longer. This should allow the people of the Gulf to have a good lifestyle for many years to come. One day, though, the oil will run out and they will need to find another way of making a living.

Kuwait is the third largest oil-producing state in the world after Saudi Arabia and Iraq. Kuwait has virtually no natural resources other than oil, and no real agriculture, but is redeveloping its traditional fishing industry.

This gas refinery in Qatar helps to process the output of one of the biggest natural gas resources in the world, known as North Field.

The Gulf state of Qatar has huge resources of natural gas, a fuel which is becoming increasingly important.

Bahrain has less oil than its neighbours, but has built oil refineries, and acts as a commercial centre. It is an island attached to Saudi Arabia by a causeway. Islamic restrictions on entertainment are less strictly enforced in Bahrain than Saudi Arabia. Because of this, the island has become a centre for relaxation and entertainment for Saudi residents.

Shi'ite Muslims demonstrate in Manama, the capital of Bahrain. Some Shi'ites feel victimized by Bahrain's Sunni ruling family and government.

The United Arab Emirates makes only a third of its income from oil, and is putting more effort than its neighbours into developing other sources of business and wealth, such as tourism. Finally, Oman, with its few natural resources, is the state which has the least oil. To improve the lives of its citizens, Oman will need to find different sources of income.

One problem faced by some rulers of Arab Gulf states is that some of their people are Shi'ites, like the majority of people in Iran. Many Shi'ites are amongst the least well-off citizens in the Gulf. Because of this, their governments fear they might one day support an Iranian-style Islamic revolution.

"Over the last 20 years, oil has helped the ruling families of the Gulf strengthen and expand their political power. In the future other global supplies of energy will undermine [weaken] this political power."
(Fareed Mohammedi, Chief Economist, Petroleum Finance Corporation, Washington, D.C.)

THE GULF COOPERATION COUNCIL (GCC)

In 1981 the six Arab countries of the Gulf, including Saudi Arabia, Kuwait, Bahrain, Qatar, the United Arab Emirates and Oman, joined to form the Gulf Cooperation Council (GCC). The GCC's initial aim was to preserve the security of the six oil-rich states and their wealth. In the Gulf crisis of 1990, however, they had to turn to the West for protection and the restoration of order.

Saudi Arabia in the 21st Century

Saudi Arabia depends on the oil industry for its wealth. Much of the country's oil is sold to the West. Linked to them by oil, Saudi Arabia has generally been able to stay friendly with Western governments, especially the USA.

The flow of oil from Saudi Arabia to the USA, and the rest of the world, has continued since the days of the oil shock of 1973. But Saudi Arabia now faces political problems, as some of its citizens seek more democracy and others sympathize with Islamic **extremism**.

After the Gulf War of 1990–1991, many US troops stayed in Saudi Arabia. This angered some Saudi Arabian Muslims. They think non-Muslim foreigners should be kept out of the Arabian Peninsula, which is home to some of Islam's holiest places. In 1995 and 1996, a total of 24 American citizens, including 19 soldiers at the Khobar barracks in Dharan, were killed in two attacks on US military targets in Saudi Arabia. From 2000 on, there has been a series of further attacks on foreigners by Islamic extremists. Soldiers, journalists and other Westerners working in Saudi Arabia have been attacked and killed.

"By arresting even peaceful reformists, Saudi authorities are proving that there is no room for peaceful action in the country."
*(Saad al-Faqih, a Saudi Islamic **dissident** spokesman resident in London)*

This photo was taken hours after the bombing of the US military residence at Khobar, in Dahran, in 1996.

Crown Prince Abdullah, a member of the Al Saud family, attends a traditional sword dance during a Saudi Arabian festival in 2003.

Most US troops were withdrawn from Saudi Arabia in April 2003, but this did little to end the anti-US feeling. The extremists are hostile to the ruling **Al Saud** family and to the West. The extremists come from all kinds of backgrounds, and are not only poor Saudis. For example, the Islamic terrorist leader Osama bin Laden is from a wealthy Saudi family.

The Al Saud family remains firmly in charge, though it has introduced some small political reforms. These include the consultative council and, in 2005, the first local elections. For now, at least, most Saudis are probably content to continue with the present situation.

POLITICAL REFORM IN SAUDI ARABIA

The Saudi government has attempted to allow people some say in its decisions, by setting up an advisory council known as the Shura Council. By 2001 this had 120 members (all men). The Shura Council is supposed to approve new laws made by ministers, and to make its own suggestions.

The Middle East and the Thirst for Oil

The world's thirst for oil will not disappear anytime soon. Some people believe more oil will be discovered. Others think there has not been enough planning for a future when oil will be scarce and expensive.

> "The Middle East will remain the largest and most important supplier of oil for decades to come."
> *(Clifford Longwell, Director, Exxon Mobil oil company)*

By 2005 oil within Western countries was running out. The USA had only 3 per cent of known oil resources. More may be found, but the quantities are unlikely to be large and it will probably be expensive to extract. In Europe the situation is similar. Known reserves of oil in the North Sea may run out by 2010, if the oil continues to be pumped at the same speed.

The result of this will be that imported oil, much of it from the Middle East, will become more important to Europe and the USA. The same will apply to the world's other major economic powers, such as China and Japan. Japan imports most of its oil from the Gulf, and China already gets a sixth of its needs from Iran.

Oil has already been at least part of the reason why wars have broken out inside and outside the Middle East. The battle for oil resources was a major factor in the Iran-Iraq war, and in Iraq's invasion of Kuwait. In Central Asia, the USA and Russia each want access to the region's oil reserves. In Venezuela, political disturbances may affect the use of the country's large oil resources.

OIL WARS

As well as the Iran-Iraq war and the invasion of Kuwait, oil has played a part in a number of other conflicts. For example, the US-led invasion of Afghanistan in 2001 has been linked to US oil interests: there are plans to build a pipeline across Afghanistan and Pakistan, to carry oil from Central Asia to the Indian Ocean. Elsewhere, Russia's war in the province of Chechnya, which wants independence, is also linked to oil resources.

For as long as the oil lasts, the Middle East will be crucial to the economies of the industrialized world. The largest resources are in Saudi Arabia, Iraq and Kuwait. The governments of each of these has strong links to the West, which has shown in the past that it will act decisively if its oil supplies are threatened. It seems likely that there will be more conflicts over oil in the years to come.

Oil rigs on and offshore in Baku, the capital of Azerbaijan, stand next to a historic mosque.

When the Oil Runs Out

Though the Middle East's oil will last for many more years, it is a limited resource and will eventually run out. It seems unlikely that the discovery of new oil resources will continue indefinitely. The Middle East will eventually have to learn to live without oil.

Some oil will be produced and bought for many years to come. Aircraft use oil, for example, and governments will be willing to pay very high prices for aviation fuel. Oil products are also the source of plastics, synthetic fibres and medicines. But generally, if more energy is needed to extract oil than can be got from it, then it is no longer economically useful.

Officials from City Hall in San Francisco, California, have bought two cars powered by hydrogen fuel cells, which do not use petrol.

ALTERNATIVE ENERGY SOURCES

At the moment, the major alternative to oil for power generation is nuclear power. Solar power, wind power and wave power are all being developed. For transport, experiments are under way with hydrogen-powered vehicles. These convert water to hydrogen and oxygen, producing energy. Some of this energy is then recovered by a hydrogen fuel cell. There are also experiments to make 'biomass' fuel from biological matter.

The Burj al-Arab Hotel in Dubai, in the United Arab Emirates. Like many Gulf countries, Dubai is working hard to attract wealthy tourists to provide an alternative income to oil.

Once the oil has run out, the West is likely to lose its **geopolitical** interest in the Middle East. Some energy experts believe this oil-less era will come as early as around 2050. Other estimates suggest that oil will last until 2100, or perhaps even longer.

Middle Eastern countries are already trying to develop other activities to take the place of the oil industry. Some are developing manufacturing or trading businesses. Others are developing tourism. Some oil money has been invested in businesses abroad, providing Middle Eastern leaders with foreign **assets**.

It is difficult to predict the future for the Middle East. With less Western interest, the region may go into an economic decline. Or, if the Middle East has been able to prepare well for an oil-less future, the oil-producing states might continue to have a strong economy in the future.

"The world is not running out of oil, at least not yet. What our society does face, and soon, is the end of the abundant and cheap oil on which all industrial nations depend."
(Dr Colin Campbell, Scientific American *magazine, March 1998)*

Glossary

Al Saud 'The House of Sa'ud' is the name of the Saudi royal family. The word 'Al' in Arabic means house or clan. This is different from 'al-', the Arabic word which means 'the'.

alliance joint military or political grouping of countries, organizations or people, aimed at bringing about a certain result

Allies in World War II, countries that were opposed to the Axis powers. The main Allies were the UK, France, the USA and the Soviet Union.

Arabian Peninsula geographical term, meaning the strip of land between the Red Sea and the Arabian Ocean. Its countries are Saudi Arabia, the Gulf states and Yemen.

asset name for anything that is the possession of a person, a business or a country

Axis powers participants in World War II that were opposed to the Allies. In 1939 the main Axis powers were Germany and Italy. Japan joined in 1940.

Ba'ath Party political party founded in Syria in the 1940s. Its aim was to give the Arabs a better future, but in practice, Ba'ath countries have been dictatorships.

barrel oil is measured in 'barrels'. A barrel is equivalent to 159 litres. The weight of a barrel varies slightly because oil of different grades varies in weight, but a rough equivalent is that 8 barrels equals 1,000 kilograms (1 tonne).

CIA (Central Intelligence Agency) agency whose duty it is to inform the US government of developments abroad, and to act in the US interest

Coalition Provisional Authority (CPA) body set up by the American-led coalition forces to govern Iraq immediately after the invasion in March 2003

concession a concession to explore for oil is an agreement between a country and a company to allow the company to search for oil and then to exploit it. In exchange the country gets benefits such as cash payments and company stock.

democracy system of government where the people regularly elect some type of assembly or administration to govern the country

derrick steel tower that stands over the head of an oil well and supports the drilling equipment

dissident person who disagrees with the policy of a government or a ruler. Usually, a dissident aims to bring about change through non-political means, sometimes including violence.

ecological concerned with the natural environment

exporting sending goods to another country to sell or use them there

extremism radical belief that refuses to accept other people's views as reasonable

federal connected with the central government of a country

free market where goods are bought and sold without any political or other restrictions

geopolitical refers to a situation where both politics and geography have an impact on relations between countries

gusher refers to the oil that 'gushes' explosively from the ground, spouting up high into the air, when a drilling rig first strikes oil

imports goods bought abroad and brought into a country

insurgent a rebel against a government or ruler. Many insurgents use violence to bring about change.

interim temporary situation

League of Nations international body set up after the end of World War I. It stopped working effectively in the 1930s, but inspired the United Nations.

mandate commission given by the League of Nations after World War I to the victorious countries, such as Great Britain, to temporarily rule conquered parts of the Ottoman Empire and former German colonies and bring them to independence as nations

military coup when an army overthrows a government

nationalist person whose political motivation is to strengthen his or her country

nationalization, nationalize when a country becomes the owner of a private company or business, previously owned either by its own citizens or by foreigners

oil reserves the total amount of oil that a country has that is still in the ground. The world's oil reserves are estimated to be more or less one trillion barrels. Some experts believe there may be more, not yet discovered.

Ottoman Empire empire based in Turkey, which ruled large areas of the Middle East until 1918

Palestine name of a territory assigned to Britain by the League of Nations as a mandate in 1920, and where the state of Israel was established in 1948

Persia, Persian Persia was the former name of the country now known as Iran. The ruler of Persia was known as the Shah.

petrochemical industry manufacturer of a range of products made using oil, including chemicals, plastics, foodstuffs and dyes

posted prices prices that were set by the oil companies for the oil they produced. The companies paid a percentage of this price to the country where the oil was produced.

production quotas amounts of oil each OPEC member state is supposed to produce

protectorate a powerful country sometimes sets up a protectorate over a weaker one in which the stronger nation has interests, to keep other countries from interfering

shares (also known as equity) equal parts into which the ownership of a company is divided, and which have been bought by the company's shareholders. By buying shares in a company, the shareholders provide it with money. Shareholders have the right to earn interest and to vote at company meetings.

Shi'ite a minority sect of Islam, which first split off from the main community after the death of the Prophet Mohammed's nephew and son-in-law, Ali. Some Muslims felt Ali and his descendants should lead the community. Others, known as Sunni Muslims, felt that the most able person should be the leader and should rule according to the traditions laid down by the Prophet.

Shura Council advisory body to the government of Saudi Arabia

sovereignty power over a country; the right to say what happens in that country and to establish law, order and government within it

United Nations (UN) all countries are members of this organization. Its job is to try to keep peace in the world.

Wahhabi, Wahhabism a fundamentalist branch of Sunni Islam that is the official faith in Saudi Arabia. The name is taken from the name of Mohammed Abdul Wahhab, who lived in the 18th century. He believed in going back to the original scriptures [of the Qur'an] to find their meaning. He also believed in extreme penalties, such as cutting off the hands of thieves.

weapons of mass destruction (WMD) refers to nuclear, chemical and biological weapons

Facts and Figures

These tables show the amounts of oil the world's main oil-producing countries are thought to have remaining (their 'reserves'), as well as the amount they pump every day.

OPEC COUNTRIES

	Reserves in billions of barrels	Production in millions of barrels per day (1 tonne = 8 barrels)
MIDDLE EAST		
Saudi Arabia	261.7	9.0
Iran	130.8	4.0
Iraq	112.5	2.3
Kuwait	96.5	2.3
UAE	97.8	2.3
Qatar	16.0	0.8
AFRICA		
Libya	38.0	1.5
Nigeria	34.0	2.3
Algeria	11.9	1.2
Gabon	2.0	0.3
OTHERS		
Venezuela	78.0	2.6
Indonesia	4.9	1.0

NON-OPEC COUNTRIES

	Reserves in billions of barrels	Production in millions of barrels per day (1 tonne = 8 barrels)
NORTH AMERICA		
USA	22.5	7.8
Mexico	18.0	3.5
RUSSIA AND EX-SOVIET UNION		
Russia	69.0	8.4
Ex-Soviet Union	27.5*	1.9
SOUTH AMERICA		
Colombia	1.7	0.5
Ecuador	4.4	0.5
NORTH SEA		
Norway	9.9	3.3
UK	25.4	2.0
MIDDLE EAST		
Oman	5.5	0.8
Syria	2.5	0.5
AFRICA		
Angola	22.9*	1.0
Sudan	1.6*	0.3

(All figures are best estimates as of 2004. *These are estimated figures, liable to be revised after further exploration.)

Timeline

1890

1892 US law requires Standard Oil to be broken up into separate companies

1900

1901 Anglo-Persian Oil formed

1908 Ford Motor Company begins production of mass market car 'Model T', laying the basis of mass demand for oil in the USA

1910

1911 British navy converts battleships to have oil-burning engines

1913 Commercial oil production begins in Iran with Anglo-Persian Oil

1914 Oil becomes a key international commodity due to demand for fuel in World War I

1920

1914 Turkish Petroleum Company agrees with Ottoman government to begin exploration in the Middle East

1929 Turkish Petroleum Company becomes Iraq Petroleum Company

1929 Standard Oil of California gets a concession to explore for oil in Bahrain

1930

1934 Kirkuk oilfield in northern Iraq begins commercial operation

1935 First oil exploration in Qatar

1938 First major oilfield found in Kuwait

1938 First major oilfield found in Saudi Arabia

1939 Oil discovered in Qatar

1940

1941 Last Shah takes the throne of Iran

1944 US oil consortium Aramco formed to exploit oil in Saudi Arabia

1945 President Roosevelt meets Saudi ruler Ibn Saud

1947 Oil exploration begins in Algeria

1950

1950

1951 Dr Mossadegh nationalizes Iranian oil. National Iranian Oil Company (NIOC) founded.

1957 First major oil discoveries in Algeria

1960

1960 OPEC founded

1962 Algeria becomes independent

1968 Iraq becomes Ba'athist state

1970

1972 Iraq nationalizes its oil industry, which is run by Iraqi oil ministry

1973 First oil shock, when OAPEC Arab oil states raise prices to Western nations

1979 Second oil shock, as prices of oil rise after Iran's Islamic Revolution

1980

1980 Start of Iran-Iraq war damages both countries' oil industries

1981 Algerian oil now 98% under state control

1988 End of Iran-Iraq war. Both countries begin to rebuild their oil industries.

1990

1990 Iraq invades Kuwait

1991 US-led coalition drives Iraqi forces from Kuwait

1991 Sanctions remove Iraq from oil market, as UN forbids Iraq to export oil

1996 UN allows Iraq to export oil for food, medicine and other essential imports

2000

2001 11 September attacks on World Trade Center in New York City. USA invades Afghanistan in October.

2003 US-led coalition invades Iraq. Iraqi oil production continues at low level

2005

Who's Who?

Bin Laden, Osama Born in 1957 into a rich Saudi family, his father made a large fortune as a civil engineer, constructing buildings in Saudi Arabia and elsewhere in the Middle East. Bin Laden came under the influence of Islamic extremists while he was a student, and went to Afghanistan to fight the occupying Soviet forces in 1979. He became a leader of an Islamic extremist group opposed to all influence in the Middle East by the USA. His organization, known as Al-Qaeda, approved, funded, and helped to plan the 11 September attacks on the USA. Following the overthrow of the Taliban regime in Afghanistan in 2001, bin Laden remained unfound.

Bush, George H. W. 41st president of the USA (1989–1993). Born in 1924, he formed an international alliance whose forces drove Iraqi troops from Kuwait in 1991.

Bush, George W. 43rd president of the USA (elected 2001, due to leave office in 2009). Born in 1946. President Bush took the decision to invade Iraq in March 2003 on the grounds that the country still had weapons of mass destruction. Some people have claimed the USA wanted Iraq's oil to be in friendly hands.

Clinton, William (Bill) 42nd president of the USA (1993–2001). Born in 1946. Clinton took some action against Iraq, notably when he launched a major air attack on Iraq in 1998. He later faced criticism for not being firm enough against Iraq.

Fahd Fahd was born in 1923, the son of King Abdul Aziz Ibn Abdul Rahman Al Saud (Ibn Saud). The fifth king of Saudi Arabia, his brothers Saud, Faisal and Khaled preceded him on the throne. In his later years, ill health compelled him to leave the day-to-day running of Saudi Arabia to his brother, Crown Prince Abdullah. Abdullah then became king upon Fahd's death in 2005.

Gulbenkian, Calouste Born in 1869 in Istanbul, and died in 1955. He was an oil entrepreneur who helped set up the Turkish Petroleum Company before World War I. He retained a five per cent interest in the company when it became the Iraq Petroleum Company and thus made an immense fortune. He moved to neutral Portugal during World War II, which then became his home.

Hussein, Saddam Hussein was born in 1937. He is the former president of Iraq. He rose to power through the Iraqi Ba'ath Party, which took full power in Iraq in 1968. Hussein became president in 1979. He started two major wars: first against Iran from 1980 to 1988, second when he invaded Kuwait in 1990, leading to the Gulf War of 1990–1991. Hussein was captured by troops of the US-led coalition in December 2003.

Ibn Saud (King Abdul Aziz Ibn Abdul Rahman Al Saud) Ibn Saud was born in 1880, and died in 1953. He succeeded his father as ruler of part of Saudi Arabia in 1901. He was internationally recognized as king in Saudi Arabia in 1932. Saud oversaw the development of the Saudi oil industry. He also held an important meeting with US President Roosevelt in 1945. He is the founder of the modern Saudi royal family.

Khomeini, Ayatollah Born in 1902 and died in 1989, Khomeini became Iran's leading cleric and was forced into exile by the Shah in 1964. Khomeini returned to Iran to found the Islamic Republic in 1979, and died after leading the country for ten years.

Roosevelt, Franklin Delano Roosevelt was born in 1882, and died in 1945. He was the 32nd president of the USA, serving from 1933 to 1945. He established close relations with Saudi Arabia and ensured the privileged place enjoyed by the USA in the exploitation of Saudi Arabian oil after World War II.

THE OIL INDUSTRY IN THE MIDDLE EAST

Western oil companies have close links with some Middle Eastern oil-producing states. In other countries, the oil industry is run by the government. These are some of the main organizations running oil industries in the Middle East:

Bahrain

The Bahrain National Oil Company (BANOCO) is owned by the Bahrain government. BANOCO in turn owns the Bahrain Petroleum Company (BAPCO).

Iran

The National Iranian Oil Company (NIOC), National Iranian Gas Company (NIGC) and National Petrochemical Company (NPC) are all owned by the government of the Islamic Republic of Iran.

Iraq

The Iraq National Oil Company (INOC) is overseen by the Iraqi oil ministry. Oil is marketed by the State Organization for Oil Marketing (SOMO). After the US-led invasion of Iraq in March 2003, the Iraqi oil industry came under the authority of the Coalition Provisional Authority. In June 2004 the Iraqi Interim Government's oil ministry resumed control. Many US and foreign companies were interested in cooperation and joint ventures.

Kuwait

The Kuwait Petroleum Corporation (KPC) is owned by the government of Kuwait. The KPC works with many foreign companies, including BP, Chevron, Getty, Exxon Mobil, Royal Dutch Shell, Texaco and Total.

Oman

The Petroleum Development Oman (PDO) owns all oil resources: 60 per cent of PDO is owned by the Omani State and 34 per cent is owned by Shell Petroleum Inc.

The Adora oil refinery in Baghdad, one of the largest refineries in Iraq.

Find Out More

BOOKS FOR YOUNGER READERS

The best resource on the Middle East for younger readers is the 'Middle East' series, of which this book is a part:

Iran and the Islamic Revolution, John King (Raintree, 2006)

Iraq Then and Now, John King (Raintree, 2006)

Israel and Palestine, John King (Raintree, 2006)

The *Making of the Middle East*, David Downing (Raintree, 2006)

BOOKS FOR OLDER READERS

The Complete Idiot's Guide to the Politics of Oil, Charles Jaco, Julianne Iwerson-Neimann and Lita Epstein (Alpha Books, 2003)
A basic guide to the politics of world oil production and how it affects the USA.

Crude: The Story of Oil, Sonia Shah (Seven Stories Press, 2004)
Sonia Shah examines the role of oil in economics and the environment.

The End of Oil, Paul Roberts (Bloomsbury, 2004)
A book that looks at what will happen when oil runs out, and why governments and oil companies behave as if it never will.

Oil: Anatomy of an Industry, Matthew Yeomans (New Press, 2004)
Yeomans looks at the history of the oil industry and shows the importance of oil in world history during the last 125 years.

Oil: Politics, Poverty and the Planet, Toby Shelley (Zed Books, 2005)
This book asks fundamental questions: notably who benefits from the production of oil, and what are the human rights and environmental issues?

ADDRESSES TO WRITE TO

If you want to find out more about oil in the Middle East, try contacting these organizations:

IN THE UK

World Petroleum Council
Fourth Floor, Suite 1
1 Duchess Street
London W1A 3DE

Energy Institute
61 New Cavendish Street
London W1G 7AR

The London Middle East Institute
Room 479, SOAS
University of London
Russell Square
London WC1H OXG

The Royal Institute of International Affairs
Chatham House
10 St James's Square
London SW1Y 4LE

International Institute for Strategic Studies
Arundel House
13–15 Arundel Street
Temple Place
London WC2R 3DX

IN AUSTRALIA

The Centre for Middle East and North African Studies
Macquarie University
Sydney 2109

The Centre for Middle Eastern and Central Asian Studies
Australian National University
Canberra ACT 0200

Index

Numbers in *italics* refer to captions to illustrations

Index